EQ

is for

EVERYONE

A look at how emotional intelligence benefits
all of us... *with examples.*

Hank Clemons

EQ

Is for
EVERYONE

Acknowledgements

To all that have graciously shared their thoughts and ideas.

TABLE OF CONTENTS

Part 1: The Foundation

Chapter 1
INTRODUCTION

This book has been written to answer the question when it comes to emotional intelligence, "Who's it for?" Over the years since emotional intelligence has made its way back into the mainstream, hundreds of books have been written on the topic. I, for one, am glad to see this level of interest in what is sometimes seen as a "warm and fuzzy" topic. This perception is slowly changing.

What hasn't changed is that most of the writings focus on "leaders" or "leadership" and their need to be or use emotional intelligence. It is said that *leaders* who are more *aware* can develop skills that will help them manage their own emotions, allowing them to respond more effectively to situations that they encounter. The better a leader relates to and works with others, the more successful he or she will be.

Further, it is said that Leaders with high-levels of social skills are intelligent communicators, develop rapport, influence, inspire vision, manage conflict and motivate others to change.

Add to that, leaders with social awareness have empathy for others and are tuned in to what others need or want. They have a higher level of team and organizational insight.

I readily admit that these are great skills to have. But, what about the rest of us?

"I'm a teller at 42nd Street Bank, can I benefit from having well developed EI (EQ)?"

"What about me?" "I'm a firefighter?" I run in and out of buildings all day or assist paramedics when there's been an auto accident."

Heyyyyyy! What about? me, "I'm an accountant ... I generally work alone and hardly ever see anyone?"

Can emotional intelligence be a benefit to these individuals as well?

Of course! It doesn't matter what's your occupation or level in the organization, having *well developed* emotional intelligence (more on this later) is an asset. As a matter of fact, you don't have to be employed at all! You can be a stay at home mom, dad, student or someone in transition.

This book attempts to communicate that *emotional intelligence is for everyone* – not just leaders. Your specific occupation or position in life may not be mentioned but the concepts and techniques can be universally applied. Having *well-developed* emotional intelligence can help all of us to more effectively handle the challenges that life throws our way daily.

■ ■ ■

Chapter 2
EMOTIONS

According to the 2002 American Heritage® Science Dictionary an emotion is defined as "A psychological state that arises spontaneously rather than through conscious effort and is sometimes accompanied by physiological changes; a feeling."

It is impossible to imagine life without emotions. Emotions are a universal part of being human. Our emotions are present during every waking moment of our life. In the work of Dr. Paul Ekman, noted Clinical Psychologist, identified seven universally expressed emotions: *anger, fear, sadness, disgust, contempt, surprise and happiness*. However, in recent years, some researchers have narrowed those six down to four - *fear, anger, happiness, and sadness*. Based on these, we build secondary emotions, which can be as many as 25.

What if you had the skills and ability to understand and channel your emotions in a healthy, positive way? What if you could guide others in managing their own emotions? We do. The key to these skills is emotional intelligence. Evidence by leading researchers and theorists in the field shows that a greater handle on emotional intelligence leads to increased productivity at work, more effective collaboration with team members, and a more positive outlook on life.

Emotions contain important information about yourself and others. Managing this information is essential to personal well-being and to building relationships. You can increase your emotional intelligence by practicing being more aware, by being more conscious of your choices, and by deliberately blending your thinking plus feeling to generate better decisions. Being "emotionally intelligent" doesn't mean "being nice," it means consciously and carefully processing and using emotional information and emotional energy.

The task is not so much to suppress emotions - every feeling has its value and significance - but to strike a balance between rational thought and emotions.

The moment you begin to value emotions as a source of information and energy, you will begin to get more positive results in your relationship with yourself and others. Everyone has emotional intelligence -- you have the chance to increase yours!

Having noticed the signs that emotions are occurring, your next step is to understand and identify those emotions. You can begin this process by asking yourself questions that will help you understand the ways that emotion has affected you. Good questions to ask include:

- What am I feeling now?
- What is this emotion trying to tell me?
- What are my senses telling me?

- What is it that I want?
- What judgments or conclusions have I made (and are they accurate)?

The answers to these questions are key to using your emotions in the service of your life goals, rather than allowing your emotions to use you.

Understanding your emotions makes it possible for you to manage them so that they work for rather than against you. By actively managing your emotions, you are taking steps towards becoming more emotionally resilient.

Here's an example of recognizing an emotion.

Let's say an engineer has come up with an amazing idea that will increase production by up to 150%, but knows his boss tends to be irritable and short-tempered in the mornings. Having emotional intelligence means that the engineer will first recognize and consider this emotional fact about his boss. Then, despite the great idea -- and his level of excitement -- he will manage his own emotions, curb his enthusiasm and excitement and wait until the afternoon to approach his boss with the idea.

Every day, emotions shape our lives and influence our decision-making. Our emotional actions and reactions affect every aspect of who we are, what we do and how we live. Understanding and having control over our emotions enables us to pursue and achieve our goals.

■ ■ ■

When dealing with people, remember you are not dealing with creatures of logic, but with creatures of emotion.

- Dale Carnegie

Chapter 3
EMOTIONAL
INTELLIGENCE

The concepts of Emotional Intelligence have been around since the early 20th century, but the term was first introduced by Wayne Payne in 1985. Nearly every profession involves human interaction. Emotional Intelligence (EI) touches and influences every aspect of our lives, from driving our behavior, making decisions, solving conflicts, the way we feel about ourselves, how we communicate with others, and how we manage everyday stress, to the way we perform in the workplace, manage, and lead teams. EI influences every aspect of our personal and professional development, helping us to advance, mature and reach our goals. Being able to manage yourself and others successfully is often a crucial factor in success.

As we know, it's not the smartest people that are the most successful or the most fulfilled in life. You probably know people who are academically brilliant and yet are socially inept and unsuccessful at work or in their personal relationships.

Improving your EI will enable you to interact and communicate with others more effectively and enhance your professional relationships. No matter what situation you're in, or what circumstance, increasing your Emotional Intelligence skills will help.

At this point, offering a definition of emotional intelligence is in order. While a plethora of definitions exist, I will share three of the prevailing ones by current thought leaders in the field. It is important to note that the definition of emotional intelligence is constantly changing as the field is still young and evolving.

1. Peter Salovey and John Mayer, developers of the MSCEIT, proposed a formal definition of emotional intelligence in 1990 as "The ability to monitor one's own and others' feelings, to discriminate among them, and to use this information to guide one's thinking and action." In 1997 this definition by Salovey and Mayer was refined and broken down into four proposed abilities that are distinct yet related: perceiving, using, understanding, and managing emotions.

2. The term emotional intelligence was popularized in 1995 by psychologist and behavioral science journalist Dr. Daniel Goleman in his book, Emotional Intelligence. According to Goleman, Emotional Intelligence is an array of skills and competencies that contribute to the performance of managers and leaders in the workplace. Those skills and competencies focus on four capabilities:

self-awareness, relationship management, self-management and social awareness.

3. Reuven Bar-On, the creator of the EQ-i 2.0™, currently published by MHS, defines Emotional Intelligence as a set of emotional and social skills that collectively establish how well we:
   a. Perceive and express ourselves
   b. Develop and maintain social relationships
   c. Cope with challenges
   d. Use emotional information in an effective and meaningful way

A couple of other definitions that are somewhat shorter but still communicates the basic idea are:

"Emotional Intelligence is being *smart* about your *emotions*"

"Emotional Intelligence is having your emotions work for you rather than against you".

'Emotional Intelligence is the skill and ability to recognize, understand and use emotions effectively".

Regardless of the definition, the general idea is that *emotional intelligence is being intelligent about your emotions*.

While definitions vary, it can be said that they all consist of one's skill and ability to be able to be aware of, control, and express one's emotions, and to handle interpersonal relationships. Let's delve a little deeper into this truly emerging field.

■ ■ ■

Emotional Intelligence is more than a term, it's a practice.

- Hank Clemons, PhD

Chapter 4
EQ VS. EI...
What's the Difference?

EQ vs. EI (Emotional Quotient vs Emotional Intelligence)

For most people the EQ and EI are used interchangeably. However, they are different and can often be the reason for ineffective emotional intelligence initiatives. Let's take a closer look at the two terms.

EQ – Emotional Quotient is the score one receives when they take an emotional intelligence test. It reflects their performance on the test. Example. Mike takes an EQ test and get a score of

120. His emotional quotient is 120. This would be much the same as someone taking an IQ test, If they scored 120, we would say that they have an IQ of 120. Their score reflects how well they did on a series of tests compared with others their age and is a measure of their reasoning and problem-solving abilities.

However, their EQ score does not reflect their skill and ability in using their emotional intelligence in dealing with their day to day interactions. One can infer that a high score indicates a high level of competence and a low score just the opposite – but does it?

Take the following scenario. Steve takes a driver's education course, then goes to the local DMV (Department of Motor Vehicles) and takes the written drivers test. He scores 99 out of a possible 100. Great score! Excitedly, he shares the results with friends. Some look in amazement but congratulates him on his performance.

A week later, he's on the local interstate and is observed by the state trooper making improper lane changes, following vehicles too closely, speeding and using a cell phone.

The state trooper signals him to pull over. With fear in his eyes and his heart pounding, he does. As the state trooper approaches, Steve wonders "what's he stopping me for?"

Ticket book in hand, the state trooper approaches the car. Upon arrival he says to Steve "Sir, do you know why I pulled you over?" Steve replies "No officer".

The trooper begins to cite the numerous infractions. Steve remembers that he still has a copy of the exam he had taken with the score printed on it. Believing that if the officer saw how he had performed on the test, he would surely not give him a citation... After all, it clearly shows that he knows how to drive and the rules of the road.

He proudly, retrieves it from the storage compartment and shows it to the officer. The officer looks at it and complements him on performing so well on the test. He then says, *"You did really on the exam – now, if only you would demonstrate it."*

His EQ (Emotional Quotient) only reflected what he knew - not if or how well he applied that knowledge.

EI (Emotional Intelligence) describes ones' skill and/or ability to recognize, understand and apply emotional information from one's self, and others.

Let's revisit the above scenario. This time however, Steve obeys the speed limit, keeps a safe distance between cars and uses his turn signals with proper distance before making lane changes. He's using/applying what he has read and learned when took the driver's education course.

Russel attends the driver's education class at the same time as Steve, However, Russel had a score of 72. But when driving on the interstate, he uses his turn signals before making a lane change, allows a safe distance between vehicles in front of him and drive at a speed that's consistent with the flow of traffic.

Even though his score wasn't as high, he applied his skills and ability more effectively than did Steve, an indication that it's not the score – EQ, but the application – EI.

In Chapter 1, I used the term *well-developed EI*. Russel exhibits *well developed* driving skills. Let's explore what is meant by this concept.

Well-Developed EI

Each emotion can exist in varying degrees of intensity or levels of arousal.

Having well-developed EI means that an individual is skilled at and knows when and how to use the different components of their emotional intelligence. As you know or will become aware, emotional intelligence consist of multiple segments depending on the model being used. In the Bar-On model, the EQ-i 2.0 assessment identifies 5 Scales and 15 Subscales that contributes to emotional intelligence. They are:

Self-Perception
- Self-Regard
- Self-Actualization
- Emotional Self-Awareness

Self-Expression
- Emotional Expression
- Assertiveness
- Independence

Interpersonal
- Interpersonal Relationships
- Empathy
- Social Responsibility

Decision Making
- Problem Solving
- Reality Testing
- Impulse Control

Stress Management
- Flexibility
- Stress Tolerance
- Optimism

5-15 (Scales and Subscales) Bar-On (EQ-i)

Another example is the ESCI (Emotional and Social Competency Inventory) by Daniel, Goleman, Richard Boyatzis and the Hay Group. The Emotional and Social Competency Inventory (ESCI) is a 360° survey designed to assess 12 competencies that differentiate outstanding from average performers. They are:

Self-awareness
- Emotional self-awareness

Self-management
- Achievement orientation
- Positive outlook
- Adaptability

Social awareness
- Empathy
- Organizational awareness

Relationship
- Influence
- Coach and mentor
- Conflict management
- Inspirational leadership
- Teamwork

ESCI (Emotional and Social Competency Inventory)

Looking at these two examples, we can see that on a scoring scale, one can be low, high or somewhere in between with each of the subscales or competencies. Most emotional assessment measures are structured in a similar fashion.

Looking back at Steve and Russel, we can see that even though Steve had a high score, his driving skills were not well developed. Russel's was - even though he had a significantly lower score. He not only knew the rules of the road, he effectively demonstrated them while driving.

Let's relate that to emotional intelligence. We'll use Steve and Russel again. This time they both attended an emotional intelligence course and took an EQ assessment as well. The results were as before. Steve was high, Russel was in the 70's.

Each are employed by similar size companies and are members of teams that provide technical support to end users of automotive parts.

Six months after attending the EQ course and getting the results on their EQ assessment, Steve's team members have been overhead to say:

"That was a waste of money, he doesn't seem to be aware of how what he says impacts others."

"When it comes to helping out around here, don't count on him".

Contrast that with the comments that's being said by Russel's team members.

"Russel always seem to know the right things to say to calm the customer's down".

"He jumps right in and helps out when we're backed up".

Russel has *well-developed* EI, Steve doesn't. Russel, through coaching or self-development, has practiced and honed the emotional intelligence components that allows him to effectively use his Social Responsibility (EQ-i 2.0 subscale) skills in helping his team members when it's needed.

He also uses his empathic (ESCI competency, EQ-i 2.0subscale) skills to effectively work with his customers and team members. Clearly a case of *well-developed* EI. More on *well-developed* EI in the chapter 6, Strategies for Developing your Emotional Intelligence.

*"**EQ** is what you know, **EI** is what you do."*
- Hank Clemons, PhD

Part 2: Emotional Intelligence in Use

Chapter 5
WHO NEEDS EI?

A straight forward answer to that question is, *we all do*. Of course saying it doesn't make it so. Often when I'm facilitating an EI workshop I'll challenge the class that if they can come up with or name an occupation where Ei is not used, I'll buy them lunch. So far, I haven't had to buy lunch – not once!

So, who needs EQ? We all do. No matter what your level in the organization or position in the company EQ is an invaluable skill.

The Occupational Outlook Handbook published by the Bureau of Labor Statistics lists hundreds of occupations and is revised every 2 years. The latest version contains employment projections out to the year 2026. Each of the occupations contains a human element. As we discussed in Chapter 1, we are *emotional being*. Therefore, the opportunity to use our emotional intelligence is virtually limitless.

Executives of multibillion dollar corporations as well as federal agencies must make decisions daily that could make or break their organizations. They must rely on more people than ever to achieve results they are personally being held accountable for by the board and stockholders. They must quickly and flexibly communicate a vision, lead system-wide organizational change, while inspiring and energizing their followers. This type of ongoing pressure can create feelings of anxiety, fear, caution, and even guilt and depression. The wrong decision or an untimely one may cause the organization or, at the very least, hamper its ability to meet its goals and objectives.

Research has shown that high EQ skills are the distinguishing characteristics that separate star performing executives from average ones. Enhancing the EQ skills of leaders enables them to lead with courage, inspire trust, demonstrate their passion, grow and retain talented leaders, and empathize with people while challenging them to meet the goals of the organization. High EQ leaders who consistently demonstrate these qualities will attract and retain talented people, thus ensuring organizational success and creating a lasting legacy.

Let's take a look at a few of the occupations and personal situations where emotional intelligence can be or is applied. We'll start with EI as a competitive advantage.

EI as a Competitive Advantage

The term is usually applied to businesses but can easily be applied to people as well. If you are an employee, work as if you were in business for yourself. That's because you are. Communicate your competitive advantage in your appearance, your resume and your interview. Once you've got the job, continue communicating your advantage in your work performance and most importantly, in the relationships you build and maintain with others.

The two main types of competitive advantages in the business world are *comparative advantage* and *differential advantage*.

Briefly, a comparative advantage refers to the ability of a business or organization that consistently produce goods and services at a lower cost than their competitors – sometimes called a cost advantage.

A differential advantage is created when an organization's products or services differ significantly from its competitors and are seen as superior.

A Model of Competitive Advantage

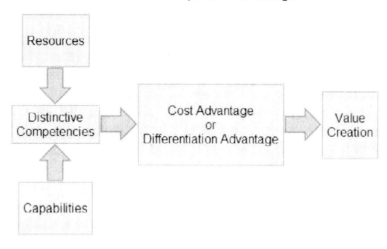

Porter, 1985

In the business world, being competitive is a must if you want to best your competition. If you simply sit around and hope that your business attracts the customers it requires to stay afloat, you will likely be disappointed.

The same can be said about you as an employee or a leader at any level in an organization. You can wait and hope that your potential will be realized among those that are technically competent, the thousand of college graduates each year, those that have "put in their time" and have organizational "seniority" or, you can develop your emotional intelligence and gain a competitive advantage.

In today's competitive job market, employers are able to look more closely at the emotional intelligence level of candidates because they can choose from a wide range of similarly qualified candidates. Your exceptional skills and abilities would serve as a differential emotional.

EI Competitive Advantage

Hank Clemons, PhD 2017

Here are some reasons why employees with well-developed levels of emotional intelligence is more important than high IQ:

- Employees with well-developed EI are more likely to stay calm under pressure
- They are empathetic to their team members and react accordingly
- They lead by example
- They tend to make more thoughtful business decisions
- They know how to resolve conflict effectively
- They admit and learn from their mistakes
- They can keep emotions in check while discussing tough issues
- They listen as much, if not more than they talk

If you want to stand out from the rest, create your competitive advantage by having a well-developed emotional intelligence.

■ ■ ■

Employers Want EI

Employers have always faced the challenge of motivating (EI) their employees and hence, those who don't need to be motivated are highly valuable in the workplace. In the business world, emotions can have a huge impact on the overall morale, productivity and job performance of employees. Emotions in the workplace are essential indications of a positive or negative job environment. Positive emotions can increase worker motivation and performance, while negative emotions can cause stress and high turnover or absenteeism.

Whether you call it emotional intelligence, emotional maturity or simply knowing how to "get along," you want employees to have the communication and organizational skills necessary to assure that they make sound decisions as they interact with fellow employers inside the organization or employers from other organization.

EI can help you to gain new perspectives on past issues, therefore improving your problem solving and decision-making abilities. It can also help with developing your strategic thinking capability and your ability to motivate and inspire others weather in a leadership position or not.

EI can help you to gain new perspectives on past issues, therefore improving your problem solving and decision-making abilities. It can also help with developing your strategic thinking capability and your ability to motivate and inspire your others.

Leaders with high skill levels of emotional intelligence have an advantage over their less skilled counterparts. EI can help you to develop empathy and understanding about other people and this is crucial when looking to inspire, influence, motivate, and persuade others in a management or leadership role.

By understanding your emotions and how to manage them, you're better able to express how you feel and understand how others are feeling. This allows you to communicate more effectively and develop stronger and more meaningful relationships, both at work and in your personal life. A good tip is to see everyone as someone you can build a work relationship with – and that includes administrative help – especially administrative help. Here's a story to illustrate what I mean.

Mike had been wanting to get an appointment to see Jim Steel, the hiring manager of Zebra Electronics. However, he did not have his direct line (phone), He did have his email address, but Jim's administrative assistant, Sally, had the responsibility of screening Jim's emails, phone calls and deciding which were answered, passed on to Jim and which went to "junk mail".

Jim receives a large volume of emails as well as "snail mail" and phone calls each day. Having someone to screen them was not only important, it was necessary as it allowed him to focus on the important "to do" aspects of his job.

Sally had been in this position for four years and knew her boss's "likes and dislikes" very well. Her EI was well developed and Jim counted on her ability to be a great "gate keeper".

Mike also had a well-developed EI and realized that if he wanted to see Jim, it would be necessary to first establish a relationship with Sally – one that would be built on trust and compassion.

On Mike's next call to Jim, he tried a different approach. He began by focusing on Sally – finding out how her day was going, how long she had worked for the company, what she enjoyed most about her job. He did not ask to speak to Jim but said that while his intention was to speak with Jim but that he had such an enjoyable conversation with her that the time he had set aside had flown by so quickly and that he needed to get back to the project that he was working on.

After doing this a couple of more times, on his third time he was put through to Jim. Sally had become his advocate and had spoken to Jim, telling him about this person that had called in on several occasions and had come across as being very personable, compassionate yet assertive and seem to be very socially responsible. She told Jim that she thought this person would be a good fit for the organization. Jim's response was, "The next time he calls, put him through." Well, you can guess what happened after that.

■ ■ ■

EI in the Legal System

Until recently, the legal community took an adversarial approach to resolving issues. Further, emotions were seen as weakness in any strategy that was being proposed. "Weak", "soft". Were just a couple of the ways that emotions was viewed by lawyers and mediators. That is no longer the case. More and more emotional intelligence is finding its way into the legal system.

For example, William L. Dawson, Administrative and Presiding Judge of the East Cleveland Municipal Court creates & conducts probation programs and educational seminars for community members and youth. He has recently added yoga and teaches it to offenders right in the Courtroom where the offenders were sentenced.

He says, "As Judge of the East Cleveland Municipal Court, I am dedicated to being a 'Cycle Breaker'." I will fight to change the careless attitude about destruction of our communities and the destruction of people's potential and futures. How will I fight? By educating people on the principles of "Finish First" and "Emotional Intelligence." He goes on to say, "My goal is to empower people so that they will start caring about their future and creating their best life before it's too late."

Then, there's mediation. The primary role of the mediator is to mediate from a position of impartiality, having no vested interest in the outcome of a dispute between parties. Another pivotal role of the mediator is to listen.

Why Deal with Emotions?

- All forms of mediations have emotions
- Most conflict is about relationships
- Failure to address emotions can stall the process

- Emotions affects perceptions how a person understands another's position, statements or needs.

Anyone who has had to resolve conflict, motivate others, negotiate, propose change or deal with people on a day-to-day basis knows how much "moods" and "emotions" affects cooperation and decisions.

Emotional Intelligence serves to improve the process of mediation by enhancing mediator awareness. Learning the skills of mediation is not sufficient which can be related to having IQ but not EQ. Both are need. This is never more evident than in the mediation process where both parties are emotionally charged plus the mediator brings his/her emotions to the conference.

The mediator assists and guides the parties toward their own resolution. The mediator does not decide the outcome, but helps the parties understand and focus on the important issues needed to reach a satisfactory resolution. Here, the mediator is employing EI skills such as assertiveness, empathy, interpersonal relationship as well as self-regard and decision making.

Generally, mediations start with a joint session used to set the ground rules and an agenda. During this session, a mediator with well-developed EI will be should be aware of their own emotion and use the emotional regulation skills to manage them so that they do not influence or interfere with the process.

Each party will usually be emotionally charged – ready to assert their reasons as of why they should prevail. The joint session also helps define the issues and determines the parties' positions.

Throughout the mediation process, the mediator offers creative approaches and innovative solutions, while maintaining an unbiased perspective. A mediator with well-developed EI will effectively use their Reality Testing skills to acknowledge their biases but not allow those biases to work their way into the mediation process.

Consider how emotions might play in highly charged legal disputes. Mediation can stall - even fail because the individuals in conflict lack self-awareness and what is actually motivating their actions. While brief, the following is an example.

Jim and Mike, two members of a work team are having an ongoing dispute over a work process. Their arguing and lack of cooperation is causing deteriorating team performance. Jim has been with the company for 8 years. Mike has only been with the for 2 years but worked in a similar position for a competitor. HR was called in and has asked that they attend mediation. They both agree.

As a mediator, learning to deal with the emotions of others is not simple. Recognizing your own feelings and considering the feeling of others is the core of emotional intelligence. It is important to understand your emotions first before you can understand other people's emotions. Learning to control your emotions with emotional intelligence is really balancing the internal feelings with the external environment.

Learning to control your emotions takes patience with yourself. It requires that you understand your feelings and are honest with yourself and those around you. Recognition of human emotion and affective expression is influenced by many factors, including culture.

It all boils down to this. People decide whether to cooperate or not. Decisions are the results of both logical considerations (facts) and emotional favor or disfavor (feelings). Therefore, if we want others to cooperate and share our convictions, we must know how to appeal to their heads and hearts together.

Emotional Intelligence (EI) is an important skill that should be a part of the ongoing development and competence of the mediator. The mediator's EI is what provides the mediator with a sense of timing, knowing when, and when not, to intervene during an unfolding conflict. Until we develop emotional self-awareness, we will project our own unrecognized emotions onto others. Mediators with well-developed EI can also be positive role models for the parties and can help the parties move more positively through the process towards a positive outcome.

■ ■ ■

Higher Ed

For decades, education focused on developing students' academic intelligence but not their emotional intelligence. In recent years however, educators and researchers have begun to realize that developing students' emotional intelligence may be just as important. Sounds familiar? There's more. It was once thought that your education was the best measure of your potential and predictor of your success. You only needed to graduate college with good grades and land a good job. However, many students' graduate college at the top of their class and still lack the emotional skills needed to be successful in their career.

According to Dr. Rachel Tustin in her course: The Importance of Emotional Intelligence in Education, states that there is a strong correlation between students' emotional intelligence and their classroom behavior. Students with low emotional intelligence may struggle to focus and have relationships with their peers or may even show aggression. Students with lower emotional intelligence tend to struggle to communicate their feelings with their peers, and this can result in struggling to form friendships with classmates or even relationships with adults.

Aggression is a common issue with students with low emotional intelligence, because they don't have the skills they need to communicate or manage their emotions appropriately. These behavior problems typically surface in preschool and early elementary school and increase in seriousness from that point on. Former UCLA administrator Chip Anderson noted, "more students leave college because of disillusionment, discouragement, or reduced motivation than because of lack of ability or dismissal by school administration." The use of Emotional Intelligence to aid the student development process can address these non-academic challenges.

In a 2014 article "Why college freshmen need to take Emotions 101" by Valerie Strauss of The Washington Post Answer Sheet, shares the following – "A 2013 survey of over 123,000 students across 153 campuses confirmed that over half of students feel overwhelming anxiety, and about a third experience intense depression, sometime during the year. Almost a third report that their stress has been high enough at some point to interfere with their academics—lowering their grades on exams or courses or projects—and 44% say that academic or career issues have been traumatic or difficult to handle. The majority of college students don't get enough sleep, and half say that they've felt overwhelmed and exhausted, lonely or sad sometime during the year."

In an article by UNCC 49'er in its Career Planning section referenced a survey that detailed what skills and traits employers want in entry-level employees. They were:

1. The ability to learn on the job
2. Listening and communications skills
3. Adaptability and creative responses to setbacks and obstacles (problem solving skills)
4. Personal management, confidence, motivation to work toward common goals, a sense of wanting to develop one's career and taking pride in their accomplishments
5. Group and interpersonal effectiveness, cooperativeness and teamwork, skills in negotiating disagreements
6. Effectiveness in the organization, wanting to make a contribution, leadership potential
7. Competence in reading, writing, and math

When you look at this list only one of the seven listed is academic. The other six traits fall under emotional intelligence. Also, a closer examination of the skills and traits desired by employers in the survey reveals that most are not centered around the individual, but one's ability to work with a team and as an employee to meet the needs of the company. For example, remaining calm under pressure, listening, and empathy are all critical skills required to be an emotionally intelligent employee.

College students are often under a great academic pressure and it can be easy for them to neglect their emotions. Well-developed emotional intelligence in college students can help them learn to manage stress and respond to peer pressure in healthy ways. It will also help them feel confident about advocating for their own needs and help them understand complicated social and workplace scenarios. For example, an emotional outburst during a class discussion will likely discourage conversations with other students, whereas, a balance of logic and controlled emotion will result in a response that encourages a robust discussion and connections with others.

Managing ones' emotions is extremely important to maintain psychological well-being during the stressful undergraduate years. Long term psychological well-being as well as psychological status during examinations is likely to affect an individual's academic performance.

Some key areas to examine and develop include:

- **Self-Regulation** – Learn your emotional triggers and methods to control them.
- **Empathy** – Understand and accept that the emotions of others are just as important as yours are to you.
- **Communications** – Communicate clearly, specific, and without emotional interjection.
- **Acceptance of Criticism** – It will certainly come and can leave you emotional charged.
- **Teamwork and Collaboration** – You must get along with and work well with others, even if you don't like them.
- **Resolve Conflict Positively** – Conflict will occur and an emotional response without thought can makes it worse.

- **Interpersonal Relationships** – With your co-workers, your boss and the people in your life.
- **Learn Body Language** – You communicate with your body language and so do others. Learn what is important to do, not to do and how to read it.
- **Learn to Deal with Stress** – As a college student you already know about stress. Stress can take a physical and emotional toll. Learn ways to cope with it, overcome it and use it to your advantage. The stress felt during exams is a natural reaction for your mind to get in the "preparation and performance mode" much like a speaker before they go on stage or an athlete before the big game.

Being emotionally intelligent does not only help students to learn better but it also determines their career success, especially for those who want to embark into a profession that requires high level of emotion related competence, such as teaching, acting or ministry to name a few. Teaching, as an example is high in emotional labor. Emotional labor refers to "the extent to which a worker must express appropriate emotions to excel in his or her job".

Not Just for Students

Whether it's at the administrative or school board level, K-12 teachers or academic faculty having a well-developed emotional intelligence is a must. For those in a position of leadership in schools, having a well-developed EI can help with facilitating and leading diverse populations. By its nature, a leadership position involves being able to garner trust and develop rapport with a variety of people. Effective leaders can identify and articulate their own feelings as well as those of others. This way, they can adjust their leadership style accordingly to meet the needs of the groups they work with.

For example, a K-12 teacher in a PTA conference would need to interact effectively with the parents. Especially in situations where the student may have behavioral issues or low academic performance. Having a well-developed EI in empathy, interpersonal relationships and assertiveness would be an important skill to employ.

According to Dr. Charles Coco, professor at Tuskegee University in a 2011 paper published in the Journal of Higher Education, he states, "Emotional intelligence has strategic implications within higher education. Academic leaders have a major role to fulfill within the administrative domain. These individuals need to manage complex situations through effective planning, organizing, leading, and controlling. They have to respond effectively to various organizational stakeholders both inside and outside their respective institutions. Individuals in positions of academic leadership could benefit from learning more about the role emotional intelligence has in organizational success."

To further illustrate this point, Michael P. Lillis, Chair, Business Department, Medaille College in his 2011 research article - Faculty Emotional Intelligence and Student-Faculty Interactions: Implications for Student Retention - found that frequent student-faculty exchanges significantly impact a student's desire to stay in college and that student faculty interactions predict student attrition intentions more strongly for those students assigned to faculty mentors who possess higher levels of emotional intelligence than for those assigned to faculty with lower emotional intelligence scores.

Having spent more than a decade as a professor teaching in both California and Florida, my experience is that being an effective instructor does not solely depend on your intellectual quotient (IQ); it also depends on how well you can use your emotional intelligence (EI). I have observed that not every student learns through the same methods, is motivated in the same manner, or acts in the same way in a classroom.

A major part of emotional intelligence is showing empathy. Try to put yourself in your student's shoes and remember what it was like when you were learning a new concept and how it made you feel. Recall your experience as a student. How empathetic was the professor? Did they often come across as if they were made of stone – unfeeling and inflexible? There's an EI opportunity here.

The more emotionally intelligent you are, the better equipped you will be as a leader of students or faculty to use their emotional intelligence in the learning arena. Increasing your emotional intelligence can lead to a better learning environment for everyone.

■ ■ ■

Any person capable of angering
you becomes your master.
*   - Epictetus*

EI and Conflict Management

In the workplace and in our personal lives being emotionally intelligent is an essential component to building resilience for mental health and successfully managing change.

Conflict will occur, and an emotional response makes it worse. Today's workers are faced with greater, and potentially riskier, challenges than ever before. Opposing points of views, coupled with high levels of stress, can lead to anger, conflict and confrontation between people, both at work and home. The heavy cost inflicted on organizations due to low morale, absenteeism, lack of cooperation and poor productivity can be devastating.

When people work together; conflict is often unavoidable because of differences in work goals and personal styles. Perhaps the most common form of conflict occurs in interpersonal encounters. Conflict can cause lost time, resources, and efficiency in any work team. But when managed well, conflict can result in new ideas, more informed decision making, and better performance. These days every organization must train its employees to effectively manage conflict and resolve issues that block performance.

What role does EQ play in managing conflict? Many people let their feelings and emotions become a major influence over how they deal with conflict. Conflicts can also occur because people ignore their own or others' feelings and emotions. Other conflicts occur when feelings and emotions differ over a particular issue.

When we are in a heighten state of agitation or anger, our decision making is compromised. Let's see how in the following situation.

Steve Walker is the supervisor of an R & D department in a major U.S. automaker. Harry Colton and Dave Smith are engineers in the R & D department.

John has a new project to complete the design of a new gas efficient automobile engine. He knows that Harry and Pete are his best two engineers and would like them to work on the project. He also knows that they don't exactly get along. Each like to do things "their way".

The emotionally intelligent leader will demonstrate empathy by making time available to talk to each employee, by listening carefully, and by asking questions to make sure that he or she understands the situation.

Begin by allowing each party to express their point of view. The purpose of the exchange is to make sure both parties clearly understand the viewpoint of the other. Make sure each party ties their opinions to real performance data and other facts, where possible. This is not the time to discuss; it is the time to ask questions, clarify points for better understanding and truly hear the other's viewpoint.

To build and maintain a model work environment, resolving conflict is at the top of the list. Teams, work groups and individuals are required to work together to carry out the mission of the organization. In any conflict situation, the relationship we have with each other as well as what we need from the conflict situation is at the forefront.

Therefore, we need to focus on building and maintaining a strong, positive relationship as well as both parties receiving maximum benefit from the conflict situation. Therefore, we encourage the use of the *Relationship/Outcome* model of conflict management. Remember, the objective is for both parties to strive to reach the highest point on the **Relationship** scale while simultaneously resolving the conflict so that it benefits both parties at the highest point on the **Outcome** scale – not an easy task.

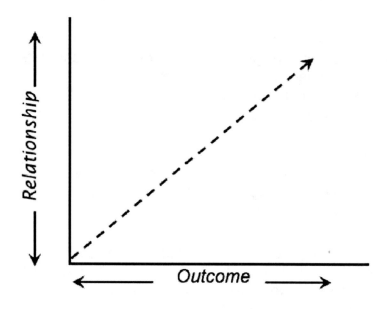

Relationship/Outcome Model

Workplace conflict is a given. Managers need to be able to differentiate between unnecessary conflict and resolvable conflict and then implement an effective problem-solving approach in each circumstance.

Model the behavior you want to see from others. There is nothing more powerful for employees than observing the "boss" do the actions or behaviors they are requesting from them.

Guidelines for Resolving Conflict

Here are some suggested guidelines that all parties must agree to in order for the conflict management process to proceed. If they don't, the process will quickly deteriorate as people try to "win" as much as possible and "lose" as little as possible.

1. Agree that now is not a good time to attempt to resolve the conflict. Allow "prime time" when energy is high, and motivation is positive, not when you are angry or tired.

2. The goal of resolving conflict is deeper understanding, not "I win; you lose." There must be an underlying attitude of respect, caring, forgiveness and no harm.

3. Check verbal weapons to be sure they are not deadly (no threat, no harm). Do not use a "battering ram" when a simple "knock on the door" will do.

4. Discuss the specific issue or specific *behavior*, not the person, personality or motivation.

5. Stay in the *present*; do not engage in coercion or fault-finding from the past.

6. Provide "face-saving" mechanisms. Don't corner the other person. Allow a "time out" if emotion gets too heavy. Then set a time to resume again.

7. When you have come to terms, put the disagreement away until you agree that it needs more discussion.

8. Triangulate. Separate people from the problem. This is not something you do only once and forget about it, it requires continuous work. The best approach is to deal with the

people as human beings and deal with the problem on its merits, or the underlying interest behind the conflict.

Our affiliations with people in personal and professional aspects do not always run smooth. Demonstrate emotional intelligence during conflicts by properly responding to and facing any dispute or disagreements with others. Understand the fact that conflicts are inevitable. However, they can be managed. And when well-developed emotional intelligence is applied in dealing with it, conflicts can turn out to be productive and helpful in strengthening both work and personal relationships.

■ ■ ■

No one cares how much you know, until they know how much you care.
- Theodore Roosevelt

EI in Customer Service

In a customer service environment, the ability to empathize allows a person to provide great service and respond genuinely to others' concerns. Understand and accept that the emotions of others are just as important as yours.

Customer Service Representatives (CSRs) deal with angry, frustrated customers continuously throughout every day. They find themselves being verbally abused through no fault of their own. The customer's anger, frustration and rage can cause representatives to become nervous, disgusted, and angry themselves. If the representative does not have well-developed EI skills, the discussion may escalate and require the intervention of the supervisor. Or worse, it can cause the company to lose that customer.

An upset customer will typically tell 8 - 10 friends about the poor treatment they received. CSRs who have well-developed EI skills can easily manage their emotional reaction to angry customers, maintaining a calm, polite and sincere attitude and conversation with customers in their in-the-moment reactions. Being able to empathize with the upset customer allows for faster, more effective problem-solving and better communication.

Maintaining customer satisfaction in the face of adversity and conflict builds customer loyalty. Loyal customers tell their friends, who tell their friends, who tell... you get the idea. Higher customer loyalty leads to higher profitability.

People in sales and marketing frequently work with difficult prospects and customers. They often find themselves in adversarial situations over price, features, delivery schedules, etc. These situations can generate anxiety, fear, frustration or even outright anger on the part of both the sales person and the customer. This can lead to a vicious negative emotional cycle where sales decline, sales people become unmotivated, and customers are unsatisfied and leave.

The characteristics most useful within this type of work are going to be those relating to being able to determine and regulate the emotions and behaviors of self and others, typically through methods of persuasion. The persuasive patterns of behavior typically exhibited by highly successful sales and marketing personnel are often likely to include both verbal and nonverbal communication – such as the observation of body language and tone of voice.

The more attention you pay to your own body language and facial expressions, not only will you be able to better communicate your message, you will also become better at recognizing and interpreting the messages of others.

Enhancing EI skills allows the sales person to have more control over themselves and thus the situation. Research shows that the more "in control" and optimistic a sales person is, the higher their volume and sales dollars. Optimism leads to persistence which leads to more sales. Being able to "read" and empathize with the customer allows for faster, more effective problem-solving and better communication. Developing strong positive relationships with customers, ensures higher sales and better cooperation when problems do arise - as they surely will.

■ ■ ■

Staff, Teams, Rising Stars

The sheer volume of work that most administrative and staff must deal with is overwhelming and it's not getting any less. They support more people who travel more and need more work done with shorter deadlines for each task. New technology, new requirements, new policies and procedures, all add to the frustration. Constant minute-by-minute interruptions are the norm.

Is it any wonder they feel completely overwhelmed, worried, dejected, confused, and fearful by all the various demands and expectations placed on them? These feelings can lead to situations where staff feels paralyzed by all they have to do. Procrastination becomes evident, errors and mistakes increase, and feeling like they have no control often leads to a depressive state where complaining and absenteeism increases.

Enhanced EI skills enable people to effectively handle multiple demands, interruptions and tight deadlines. Processes, databases, and projects run more smoothly, details do not fall through the cracks, and professional staff is freed-up to focus on their work.

Whether you're a part of a team or an independent contributor, teams come in all sizes and types; self-managed, cross-functional, virtual. As a result, teams are shouldering more and more responsibility for major organizational initiatives. They are under pressure to work smoothly with people they may never see face-to-face both inside and outside their organization. Deadlines are tight, resources are scarce, technology is rapidly advancing, and team members are constantly changing.

Therefore, it's easy to be dejected, overwhelmed and confused as things change about you. It's normal to feel angry when a team member doesn't deliver, disgusted when resources are taken away, and you are still expected to meet tight deadlines.

Team cohesion can break down and progress can slow to a creep. Product introductions are missed, and market share can be lost to competitors.

Teams with well-developed EI skills can dramatically shorten the storming phase of team formation. Team members deal effectively and efficiently with their own and other member's emotional turmoil, using it as a source for developing team cohesion and trust. Major projects of significant importance to the organization are achieved on time and on budget. The organization gains a reputation as a great place to work and grow thereby continuing to draw top talent.

High EI Teams Members (Well-developed EI)

Just as team members will have an expectation of their team leader, they will also have an expectation of each team member. Being a great team member can aid the team process as much as a good team leader. Here are some of the elements that high EI team members exhibit:

- *Commitment to the team above themselves.* The factors that made up a successful team leader included both commitment to people and a desire to support and serve. High EI team members are also servant minded: seeking to serve others before their own needs.

- *Positive contribution to Team Process and Goals.* Some team members may be willing to take a back seat - saying "it's the leader's role to tell us what to do!" This is **not** the behavior of a high EI team member. High EI team members will support the team leadership with suggestions for improving the effectiveness of the team process or new ideas for delivering the team goals.

- *The 3 E's - Enthusiasm, Energy, and Expertise* High EI team members don't only want their leaders to inspire and motivate them, having other team members who are also able to play this role is seen as very positive by most team members.

- *Willingness to take responsibility for various elements of the teamwork.* Arising out of the previous element, team members should be willing to run with the ball - taking away tasks from the main group to work on. These might not only be tasks but could also include other aspects of the team project.

- *Delivering on commitments.* If an individual is to be fully valued by the team and truly a high EI team member, they must be committed to the success of the team. If they agree to carry out action steps at team meetings, there is an expectation that these will be carried out, unless that expectation is changed. If at the following team meeting, the team is surprised by an individual not delivering on what they agreed, there is a danger that they will lose trust in the individual. Further occurrences of this will almost certainly move the group process backwards – possibly to the *norming* or *storming* stage. It is better to resist the pressure to deliver initially and set appropriate expectations, than to say yes, and then spend the next weeks finding ways of apologizing.

We can conclude then that EI is very relevant in selecting members to teams. People with low EI are likely to have difficulty working on teams. Therefore, we should make every effort to assess the EI of each prospective team member prior to putting them together. If the team has already been formed, then it is strongly recommended that the entire team is trained in emotional intelligence to develop a higher performing team.

Rising Stars

Rising stars are high potential people that take on demanding multiple projects and leadership roles. Often, unforeseen events occur that can delay or derail critical business initiatives under their responsibility. They have daily contact with customers, suppliers and even competitors who are often irate and threatening.

Swamped by emails, these situations can cause the person to feel anxious, fearful and overwhelmed. They may feel frustrated that things are not moving along as they should and therefore have a negative impact on their career.

Such negative emotions can lead to poor decisions resulting in multimillion-dollar losses. Product setbacks and marketing campaigns go awry as critical details fall through the cracks. A lack of talent can keep the company from developing new products and services, crippling its chances in its industry.

Research has shown that high EI skills are the distinguishing characteristics that separate the rising stars from average ones. The earlier these interpersonal skills are developed, practiced, and internalized, the more likely Rising Stars and the company are to experience success. Ensuring that rising stars develop their EI skills to the fullest ensures that a wealth of competent leaders are available to introduce new products, start new businesses, and lead the organization through grow and expansion.

■ ■ ■

EI and Technical Professionals

Technical Professionals are constantly under pressure to do more with less, faster, better, and cheaper. They work long, hard hours to complete projects. They are challenged to create and innovate, interact with a multitude of people from different functions, and do tasks, in many cases, they would like to avoid.

These situations can cause technical professionals to be agitated, resentful, anxious, frustrated, and stressed-out much of the day. Communication is hampered, more mistakes and errors are made, and creativity is blocked.

Enhancing the technical professional's EI skills provides them with what they never were taught in school - how to manage their own emotional reactions to people and situations and how to build interpersonal skills that allow them to get other technical colleagues to help them when they need it. Strong EI skills ensure that projects are completed on schedule, and that they incorporate the best innovative thinking that is available both inside and outside the organization.

Team Leaders and Project Managers

Team Leaders and Project Managers are held accountable for setting and maintaining a positive environment where very diverse, non-local individuals can work together to achieve success in shorter and shorter time periods on projects of greater magnitude and importance. They must eliminate roadblocks and internal and external or organizational barriers, so their teams can achieve success.

Projects can easily fall behind schedule. Teams become dysfunctional or members leave causing further delays. Enhancing EI skills of team leaders and project managers enables them to maintain a positive attitude as they eliminate impediments to team success. By improving their own self-awareness and self-motivation, they motivate their team to high, sustained levels of performance and achievement. Major projects of significant importance to the organization are achieved on time and on budget.

The effect - critical talented staff are developed and retained. Successfully managing one's emotions in the workplace does not mean suppressing these emotions. Doing so only results in an increased likelihood of an emotional outburst later down the road.

Most of what we do in our professional and personal lives entails dealing with other people. Emotional Intelligence is the key to handling these relationships in an effective and harmonious manner. An important component of emotional intelligence is self-management. Emotions like anger, anxiety or frustrations, prevent us from staying focused and thinking clearly.

How many people do you know who have been fired because of lack of technical skills or low IQ? Not many, I would guess. Discounting lay-offs due to business imperatives, more employees are fired because of reasons related to lack of emotional intelligence than to deficits in IQ or poor technical skills. A study by the Centre for Creative Leadership, for example, showed the top six reasons that managers are derailed, they were:

- They used a bullying style viewed as intimidating, insensitive, and abrasive.
- They were viewed as being cold, contentious, aloof, or arrogant.
- They betrayed personal trust.
- They were self-centered and viewed as overly ambitious and thinking of the next job.
- They had specific performance problems with the business.

- They over-managed and were unable to delegate or build a team.

While none of the derailed managers had all weaknesses. Overall, their central problem was poor human relation skills; they did not treat people as valuable assets. All the weaknesses clearly fall into the four competencies of EQ.

Increasingly employers are listing "soft" skills, as a hiring requirement for jobs of all kind. And this is not just jobs that traditionally require soft skills, such as jobs in customer service or sales, but even jobs in high tech. A number of books and articles have been written on the importance of emotional intelligence as a success determinant, both for individuals and organizations - ultimately, it boils down to one important reason: it makes us better human beings.

■ ■ ■

Interpersonal Relationships

An important factor in our ability to successfully connect is emotional intelligence. When it comes to happiness and success in our relationships, career and personal lives, emotional intelligence (EI) matters. As we know, it's not the smartest people that are the most successful or the most fulfilled in life. You probably know people who are academically brilliant and yet are socially inept and unsuccessful at work or in their personal relationships.

Becoming aware of how you react to situations is priceless in accepting how you deal with situations at home and at work. Conversely, having limited awareness will lead to distractions, arguments and poor relationships. Therefore, a clear understanding and the ability to discuss matters can lead to better relationships and wellbeing. Here's an example of a typical workplace scenario.

On the work side...

Recently, you and several members of your group have become aware of personal disagreements and unspoken resentments among the group members. There is no official procedure to handle such problems, and you realize that, not only is productivity (personal and collective) suffering, but that everyone appears to be unhappy in general with the declining working conditions these problems have created. You would like to do something to improve the situation.

A situation such as this relies on your interpersonal relationship skills. Professional relationships are strengthened because there is understanding and open communication among coworkers. Emotional intelligence can help you navigate the social complexities of the workplace, lead and motivate others, and excel in your career.

Another example of what can create a "shaky" interpersonal relationship at work can happen when giving a performance review. No employee likes to receive a negative performance review. However, giving negative feedback in a review can be unavoidable based on the employee's performance during the review period.

Employees may become angry over not receiving an expected pay increase, promotion or other performance-related incentives, and may become argumentative; even lash out by spreading gossip and exhibiting a negative attitude at work. These behaviors can create sensitive situations that require tactful communication.

To resolve a conflict of this type, calls for a high level of self-awareness and social skills. Create a positive environment free from distractions. When delivering the news, begin with the end in mind – an agreement to improve. Be empathetic, you've been on the receiving end of a performance evaluation. Even if it was all positive, you had a few butterflies as you waited to hear news. Seldom does the supervisor's point of view match yours.

Work directly with the employee to create a solid, time-bound plan of action to improve their performance and tie the completion of these goals to a reward. Allow the employee an opportunity to express their emotions in a socially acceptable way. Acknowledge their emotions. Think this is important? You bet it is.

On the personal side…

The most thriving relationships consist of two people who have a sense of responsibility and understanding of their own emotions, expectations and goals. Emotional Intelligence is all about you being comfortable with self or as we say, "you're comfortable in your own skin". You should confidently be able to express your thoughts and point of view to your partner.

Healthy relationships are built around mutual understanding that involves empathy, trust and acceptance of each other's values. A 2014 article in Psychology Today titled: How to Increase Your Emotional Intelligence — 6 Essentials" by Preston Ni M.S.B.A. **offers** the following.

A. Reducing Negative Personalization. When you feel adversely about someone's behavior, avoid jumping to a negative conclusion right away. Instead, come up with multiple ways of viewing the situation before reacting. For example, I may be tempted to think my friend didn't return my call because she's ignoring me, or I can consider the possibility that she's been very busy. When we avoid personalizing other people's behaviors, we can perceive their expressions more objectively. People do what they do because of *them* more than because of *us*. Widening our perspective can reduce the possibility of misunderstanding.

B. Reducing the Fear of Rejection. One effective way to manage your fear of rejection is to provide yourself with multiple options in important situations, so that no matter what happens, you have strong alternatives going forward. Avoid putting all of your eggs in one basket (emotionally) by identifying a viable Plan B, and also a Plan C, should Plan A not work out. Example. You recently submitted a bid for a project that you felt was "just right" for you. You matched up very well with the requirements that had been stated. Winning this bid would pay off several of your debts, give you a financial cushion for at least six months and be a great reference for future bids. However, a week later you receive an email stating that you were not selected. What could be your Plan B and C in this scenario? Use the approach below to develop a Plan B and C.

    a. Increased fear of rejection: "I'm applying for my dream job. I'll be devastated if they don't hire me."
    b. Decreased fear of rejection: "I'm applying for three exciting positions. If one doesn't pan out, there are two more I'm well qualified for." (This approach is referred to as reframing. More on this later in the book)

So, if you want to develop deeper connections with friends, colleagues, or your significant other, cultivating your emotional intelligence (EQ) should be one of your top priorities.

Improve your EI and improve your success in virtually all areas of your life.

By learning to observe your thoughts and feelings without judgment, you can increase your awareness of them with more clarity, rather than having them blurred by the baggage of your assumptions. In other words, mindfulness (discussed later in the book) decreases the odds of your being unknowingly high-jacked by negative emotions.

Our life experiences and daily encounters with people and situations affect our emotions. In order to communicate well with those, we deal with, we have to be on guard with our emotions, learn to recognize them, and know how these feelings affect our actions and our relationships with others.

By taking the time to increase your EI, you can create more meaningful and productive relationships around you in both your personal and professional life. Just like a muscle you strengthen at the gym, you can learn to reprogram your brain and strengthen your "emotional intelligence muscles".

When we have well-developed emotional intelligence, we will increase our ability to develop more solid, trusting relationships in our business arena. Relationships are so important to our success in business, and not just our relationships with clients. Our internal relationships – the ones we have with our colleagues and team members – are equally as important.

Having well-developed emotional intelligence skills will increase a person's emotional awareness and a strong emotional foundation which helps develop good relationships.

So, if you want to develop deeper connections with friends, colleagues, co-workers or your significant other, cultivating your emotional intelligence (EI) should be at the top of your "To do" list.

■ ■ ■

No doubt emotional intelligence is more rare than book smarts, but my experience says it is actually more important in the making of a leader. You just can't ignore it.
                                        - Jack Welch

EI and Leadership

What is a leader, and what do they do? Most people would say, "They lead". True. However, some are effective, others are ineffective. Effective ones probably use EI, whether they know it or not, ineffective ones probably don't or as we've learned, is not well-developed.

John Mackey, CEO and founder of Whole Foods in a 2013 interview with Lewis Schiff, Director, Inc. Business Owners Council said, "I think for leadership positions; emotional intelligence is more important than cognitive intelligence. People with emotional intelligence usually have a lot of cognitive intelligence, but that's not always true the other way around".

Being the leader in a multi-million-dollar global corporation, an NFL team or in anything for that matter, is a tough job and not suited for everyone. Being a *successful* leader requires more than just assigning tasks to the team. It calls for someone who can inspire team members to achieve their full potential.

That's exactly what Jeffrey Lurie, owner of the Super Bowl LII (52) champions Philadelphia Eagles got when he hired Doug Pederson. Prior to hiring Pederson, when asked what he'd be looking for, Laurie said, "It's several things," "Number one, a smart, strategic thinker. You have to be someone looking out for the short-term, mid-term and long-term interest of the franchise."

Also, "Looking for somebody who interacts very well and communicates clearly with everybody he works with and comes in touch with. Understands the passion of our fans and what it's like to coach the Philadelphia Eagles. It's a unique and entirely passionate fanbase that just wants to win."

"You've gotta incorporate that in your life, in your heart and you have to be willing to do that. Another thing is attention to detail. I think all great coaches have tremendous attention to detail in this league."

"Lastly, you've got to open your heart to players and everybody you want to achieve peak-performance. I would call it a style of leadership that values information, all of the resources that are provided and at the same time, values *emotional intelligence*. I think in today's world of the way business are run and sports teams are run, you need a combination of all those factors to create the best chance to succeed."

This is true across the board. Leadership has changed over the past fifteen years. Command and control is no longer the prescription for successful leadership - cooperation and collaboration is. A leader must have well developed emotional intelligence to align personal and subordinate goals to accomplish company goals.

We must learn to manage emotions the same way as we manage time, equipment, and other resources. Often our uncontrolled emotions are the product of stress that has been building up over time. Left unmanaged, our emotions can continue to fuel the feelings of stress, eventually leading to short tempers, angry words and unproductive activity. While we can't always control feelings of stress, we can and therefore should try to control the disruptive emotions that they may trigger.

Consider the following:
- Pay attention to your emotions.
- Realize that emotions are a part of the workplace.
- Determine the source of your feelings.
- Express your feelings in a non-confrontational manner.
- Acknowledge the other party's feelings as legitimate.
- Request a "time out."

- Maintain a neutral body and voice.
- Focus on the positives.
- Be non-judgmental.
- Ask workers what's on their minds.
- Turn off the heat.
- Treat everyone fairly.
- Offer help when it's needed.
- Ask workers what's on their minds.

Leaders with well-developed levels of emotional intelligence have an advantage over their less skilled counterparts. EI can help you to develop empathy and understanding about other people and this is crucial when looking to inspire, influence, motivate, and persuade others in a management or leadership role.

By understanding your emotions and how to manage them, you're better able to express how you feel and understand how others are feeling. This allows you to communicate more effectively and develop stronger and more meaningful relationships, both at work and in your personal life. A good tip is to see everyone as someone you can build a work relationship with – and that includes administrative help – especially administrative help.

As leaders we often find ourselves spending an inordinate amount of time checking the work of our staff; identifying what is wrong; identifying mistakes and concentrating on errors. Well-developed EI leaders look for opportunities to find people doing things right and offer them the encouragement they need to keep on doing things right. A leader with well-developed EI will, find time in their daily schedule to do the following:

- Talk with staff, take note of and encourage their free-time activities.
- Make certain that staff members have the necessary resources to complete their tasks.

- Provide a wide variety of rewards – tangible and intangible.
- Take the time to explain to staff members that their role is integral to the success of the organization.
- Demonstrate a genuine interest in the work of staff and recognize and encourage improvement.

Emotional intelligence has become a vital part of how today's leaders meet the significant challenges they face. Emotional intelligence can help leaders in an ever more difficult leadership role, one that fewer and fewer people seem capable of fulfilling. And in the middle of the talent war, especially at the highest levels in organizations, emotional intelligence can give developing leaders a competitive edge.

Applying EI in the workplace goes beyond simply controlling your anger and getting along with others. It also focuses on learning to be self-aware, empathetic, adept and flexible in relationships. Emotional intelligent leaders possess the following 10 skills:

1. Motivate others

2. Focus on personal /organizational achievement

3. Understand others

4. Communicate efficiently and effectively

5. Lead others

6. Build successful teams

7. Handle conflict appropriately

8. Change organizations appropriately

9.   Manage diversity

10. Manage creativity and innovation

The new demands leaders have to meet.

Leaders now need to manage and lead an "empowered" workforce and go beyond the consultative, co-operative and democratic styles of yesterday. These new demands include:

- consultation and involvement – *but leaders still get criticized for not having and communicating a compelling vision and purpose*

- autonomy and freedom – *but leaders are still expected to take full responsibility when things go wrong*

- opportunities for growth, challenge and glory - *but leaders must be on hand to coach and mentor us so that we develop our potential*

- inclusion and team spirit – *but we still want our leaders to give us individual recognition and acknowledgement.*

However, there are not enough talented (i.e., super-human) individuals who can meet all these demands.

This ability – understanding what people think and feel, knowing how to persuade and motivate them, and resolving conflicts and forging cooperation – is among the most important skills of successful leaders – all clearly emotional intelligence skills.

Leaders with well-developed EI tend to do the following on a consistent basis.

- Be consistent in your delivery and expectations.
- Communicate with language that is positive, yet firm.
- Create a pleasant, safe working environment.
- Communicate with customers, coworkers and clients on a regular basis.
- Intervene early when difficulties arise.
- Teach your team/staff problem solving techniques.
- Communicate and coordinate with peers, even those in other organizations.
- Determine staff ability levels.
- Identify appropriate motivational tools.
- Maintain high supervisory mobility within the workplace.
- Involve your staff as much as possible, in day to day decisions and long-term planning.
- Articulate and arouse enthusiasm for a shared vision and mission.
- Guide the performance of others while holding them accountable.

People want to be guided by a person they respect, someone who has a clear sense of direction. Be passionate about what you do. Leaders with well-developed EI have a contagious passion for what they believe in. Imagine a basketball team who has a coach who eats, breathes, and lives by the sport, yet his team does not share in the passion. What will the result be? A team that does not play to their full potential. Why? Because they don't share the passion that their coach has. Recall years ago, when Pat Riley was the head coach of the Los Angeles Lakers. Not only did he have a passion for winning but so did the players such as Magic Johnson, Michael Cooper, Kareem Abdul-Jabbar, James Worthy, and Byron Scott. The same can be said about the Golden State Warriors.

The same applies in business. When your team members are passionate about the success of your company, they not only enjoy their work, but they want to contribute to the company's success. This passion also reduces the level of employee turnover.

Characteristics of Leaders with Well-Developed EI

A leader with well-developed EI knows how to appreciate differences. Instead of fighting over people's differences, a leader with well-developed EI knows how to utilize different people's strength and talent to strengthen his/her organization.

A leader with well-developed EI knows how to motivate him/her self. One of the main reasons why so many people are not successful in what they do, it's because they are unable to motivate themselves. Life is full of challenges and trials, but our ability to deal with our disappointments and to motivate ourselves when we have been knocked down will determine the level of success.

A leader well-developed EI treats other people as if they are important – because they are. Everybody wants to be treated with respect and they want to be appreciated. People want to know that their self-worth is important, and a leader with well-developed EI knows how to show a genuine appreciation & complement toward other people.

Listen. A leader with well-developed EI listens when their team members speak to them about all their work-related worries (and some not work related), hear them out. You could convey empathy, suggest alternatives and create harmony within the team.

James A. Vena in his book, The Entrepreneur's Edge: Tapping into Your Inner Entrepreneur says, "If the only life you're focused on improving is your own, then you are probably missing the point on what it takes to be a real leader! True leaders develop and empower others".

■ ■ ■

EI and Followership

Employees now have far more options and choices than the foot soldiers of yesterday. Management gurus and leadership experts have written volumes on leaders and the theories of leadership. However very little has been written about the qualities of these unknown soldiers who commit their hearts and souls to achieve their leader's goals. Almost every leader in one way or the other owes his/her success to these followers. Without their help no leader can achieve success.

High EI followers don't just *do* their time—they spend their time *doing*. Rather than complaining about what's not right, what's not working, what's wrong with this place, they get involved in helping the cause. High EI followers are loving critics. If they don't like the way things are being done or the direction the company is headed, they get engaged in proposing new ideas and searching for solutions. They maintain an active role and are clear about what they can do to make a difference, and then get on with doing it.

The good news is, all of these skills can be learned. Becoming follower with well-developed EI skills at work is like improving your golf or tennis game. You identify your bad habits and the improvements you need to put in place - and then you practice those improvements every day.

A good follower exemplifies the same qualities as those of a leader and that is being a good listener: someone who listens and responds with full attention rather than simply waiting for his or her turn to speak. Since we discussed the qualities of a good listener in the previous chapter, we hesitate to present them again. Instead, let's explore some other aspect of high EI followers.

- Demonstrating respect

- Thinking win/win
- Working within the system
- Acting proactively
- Appreciating differences
- Striving toward a common goal (one shared with leaders)
- Recognizing any authority that leaders may possess
- Tailoring actions to accord with leaders' ideals
- Making decisions based on a set of values
- Enthusiastically working towards organizational goals while nevertheless remaining accountable for results
- Gaining the trust of leaders
- Fostering enough independence to allow followers to achieve goals without complete reliance on leaders
- Requiring only high-level guidance
- Demonstrating effectiveness when working in a group independently
- Recognizing the hierarchy of leadership while becoming a self-motivated mini-leader
- Proactively working to fulfill or exceed expectations

Followers lead by example within their companies just as leaders do – this is how high EI organizations are born. They are often leaders in their families, communities and social organizations. Both require loyalty, dependability, and unselfishness.

More and more firms are encouraging followership to improve company performance. High EI followers are highly capable self-managers who require minimal supervision--a real cost-saving benefit. They feel involved and responsible for their own work, which makes them more productive. High EI followers are stimulating people to work with. Their commitment is *contagious*. If you're not one now, you can be!

Emotional Contagion

Emotional Contagion is a process in which a person or group influences the emotions or behavior of another person or group through the conscious or unconscious induction of emotion states and behavioral attitudes.

Emotional Contagion-Team

The group's emotional state has an influence on factors such as cohesiveness, morale, rapport and the team's performance. For this reason, organizations need to take into account the factors that shape the emotional state of the work-teams, in order to harness the beneficial sides and avoid the detrimental sides of the group's emotion.

Managers and team leaders should be even more cautious with their behavior, since their emotional influence is greater than that of a "regular" team member. It has been shown that leaders are more emotionally "contagious" than others.

Emotional Contagion-Customer Service

The interaction between service employees and customers is considered an essential part of both customers' assessments of service quality and their relationship with the service provider.

Positive affective displays in service interactions are positively associated with important customer outcomes, such as intention to return and to recommend the store to a friend.

It is the interest of organizations that their customers be happy, since a happy customer is a satisfied one. Research has shown that the emotional state of the customer is directly influenced by the emotions displayed by the employee/service provider via emotional contagion. But, this influence is dependent on the degree of authenticity of the employee's emotional display, such that if the employee is only surface-acting, the contagion of the customer is poor, in which case the beneficial effects stated above will not occur.

■ ■ ■

Instead of resisting any emotion, the best way to dispel it is to enter it fully, embrace it and see through your resistance.

- Deepak Chopra

Part 3: Improvement Strategies

Chapter 6
DEVELOPING YOUR EI: 5 Strategies

Where do I Start?

It starts with Self-Awareness. Self-Awareness is the skill of being aware of and understanding your emotions as they occur and as they evolve. None of us are perfect. The more you know about yourself, the better you'll be able to understand how you're perceived by others and why they respond to you the way they do.

We all have fears, self-doubts, inadequacies, and insecurities we don't want others to know about. In most cases we may not want to admit them to ourselves. Building this awareness can not only help you thrive in a corporate setting and enjoy happiness in the workplace, but also lead to a more effective and satisfying life in general.

Working effectively with members of your team, peers and management at all levels is key to your success and to the success of your organization. Yet how can we effectively communicate with; effectively work with individuals and groups with diverse working styles and preferences? A foundation of professional success lies in self-understanding, understanding others and knowing the impact of one's personal behavior on others.

Many of us avoid self-awareness. We want to protect, maintain, and enhance our self-concept and the images others have of us. We have fears, inadequacies, self-doubt, and insecurities that we don't want to reveal to others or even admit to ourselves. If we open ourselves up to honest self-appraisal, we might see things we don't want to see. None of us are perfect and knowledge about our strengths and weaknesses can help us gain insights into areas we want to change and improve.

Developing your emotional intelligence requires *time* and *practice* – two areas most of us don't have enough of or resist doing. Most of all it requires a serious examination of your emotional behavior, how you interact with others and recognizing areas you need to improve in.

A first step to improve your EI would be to work on how you perceive your own emotions. If you know how you feel in certain situations and why you feel that way, it will become much easier for you to understand other people's emotions. This is called Self-Awareness – one of the four components of the model developed by Daniel Goleman.

What's My Current EQ?

While this seems like a question that everyone should ask, you might find it surprising that few people ask it. Often people will simply look for a course that will teach them about emotional intelligence. Much like the individual that applaud because everyone else is applauding

I suggest before taking a course, you should answer the question "Why do I want/need to develop my emotional intelligence". Reasons could include:

- Improve personal relationships
- Improve professional Relationships
- Be a better friend
- Be a better husband/wife
- To be more empathic
- To be a better leader
- Be better at communicating with others
- To get a better job
- To be a better team member
- To perform better as a student
- To improve my overall wellbeing
- To lead a healthier, happier and more productive life

There can be a multitude of reasons. I encourage you to identify the top three – write them down. They will be where you focus. You may discover as you move along that they might change or blend into one.

After answering the "Why" question. The next question is "Where am I now". This question is asked to identify your strengths and challenge areas. You will get a snapshot report of where you fall relative to other people. This information is meant to give insight, not to paint a picture that is unchanging but as a living canvas that can be view differently depending on where you're standing (context).

Far too often when an individual receives their scores from an EQ assessment, they become "fixed" on the score and see it as defining them. I tell my clients to think of it as taking a 'selfie". I then walk over and stand next to them as if we're taking a "selfie". I then walk away and ask if the imaginary photo is representative of us now or five minutes earlier. The answer is usually "no".

Assessing your EQ

As discussed earlier, many models and definitions of EQ have been proposed. The same holds true for tools that measure emotional intelligence.

Currently no test can measure EQ as precisely as IQ. However, the EQ-I 2.0™ by MHS is the one I use most often with my clients. As a Training Partner with MHS, I facilitate certification training for others to be approved to use this highly rated and validated tool. Without a doubt it's at the top of my list.

My alternate assessment is the EISAP 2.0™ which I developed several years ago and recently updated. This assessment consists of 40 questions/statements that are based on the four core competencies discussed earlier – Self Awareness, Social Awareness, Self-Management and Relationship Management. The emotional intelligence test will evaluate several aspects of your emotional intelligence and will suggest ways to improve it.

For more information on either of these assessments, see the contact information at the back of this book.

Having assessed your EQ, and settled on and area for development, let's explore 5 strategies that can be applied to a variety of emotional intelligence issues.

■ ■ ■

Strategy #1

Reframing

Reframing is a way of viewing and experiencing events, ideas, concepts and emotions to find more positive alternatives. Reframing involves identifying our unhelpful thoughts and replacing them with more positive or adaptive ones. Reframing is thinking about a current perspective in a new and different way.

Reframing is also an opportunity to rethink the event or story in a more positive light. This is important because how we see a person, situation or challenge impacts on how we respond.

Our minds are constantly bombarded with negative thoughts, visions of horrible things that may happen to us, and terrifying reasons not to do the things we want to do - yet in the end, these horrible things rarely ever happen.

For example, a job seeker that failed to get a job after an interview might have self-talk that sounds like this:

"I blew it!"

"They weren't going to hire a woman for that position."

"They wanted someone younger/older."

"The interviewer didn't like me because I wasn't tall enough."

"I was too nervous."

Instead, they might reframe the self-talk by telling themselves that it was a "useful learning experience". Or in the example above, instead of blaming ourselves for being *nervous*, remind ourselves that being nervous might be a very normal and helpful response in a given situation?

Instead of bottling up emotions, try acknowledging your feelings while reframing your thoughts to stay positive even in trying situations. For example, if you get "called on the carpet" at work, acknowledge that you feel disappointed or discouraged, but also tell yourself truthfully that this situation is a learning opportunity, not only in terms of your work product, but also in terms of having crucial conversations with your boss.

A reframe is far more effective when you understand what's going on behind the thought (Emotional Self-Awareness).

To effectively reframe, there are three things to remember.

The first one is that events or situations do not have inherent meaning; rather, we assign them a meaning based on how we interpret the event.

For example, something seemingly horrible happens to you, *it is only horrible because of the way you look at it*.

Examples you can reframe:
- A weakness as a strength
- A problem as an opportunity
- Unkindness as lack of understanding

Here's one that most of us have heard.

Statement: "We've tried that already and it doesn't work."

Reframe: "So, we have a good idea about what doesn't work. What can we do differently this time?"

Think about what other understandings or viewpoints might be possible. Try to suspend judgments and remain curious about different ways to understand the person, event or challenge.

Use reframing to develop:
- Self-Regard
- Assertiveness
- Independence
- Reality Testing
- Optimism

Reframing can be used to help remove limiting beliefs, to help appreciate positive moments that you might otherwise miss, or for any other negative thought you would like to change.

■ ■ ■

Strategy #2

Journaling

Journals help you improve your self-awareness. If you spend just a few minutes each day writing down your thoughts, this can move you to a higher degree of self-awareness. Journaling, also called reflective writing, allows you to be aware of your own thoughts and feelings and be in a better position to manage and handle stress.

Journaling is a practice through which individuals can work on improving their own emotional self-management and emotional intelligence by documenting their life experiences and the different emotional changes they experience as a result of these events on a daily basis. In doing so, individuals are able to work through their emotions in a private, personal, and productive manner. Periodically, look back over your journal and take note of any trends, or any time you overreacted to something.

In my practice as an emotional health and wellbeing coach, I give each of my clients a small spiral notebook and ask them at the end of each day to record at least five emotions that they experienced. Then reflect on the action taken based on those emotions and answer the question as to whether it was appropriate or not for the situation. We need to understand why we feel in particular ways and what these feelings mean for us. Then we are able to change negative emotions into positive ones.

Here's are 5 simple proven steps to keeping a journal.

1. Close your eyes and take several deep breaths and 'feel' what you are feeling.
2. Think about what the names for your feelings are.
3. Then begin your sentences with...... **Today I feel**..........
   sad, mad, troubled, uncertain, happy, excited, frustrated, embarrassed, angry, etc.
4. Then write "Why am I feeling this?"
5. Then answer as many of the following as possible.
   a. How often do I feel like this?
   b. Where did the feeling come from?
   c. When have I felt like this before?
   d. How can I change the feeling around?
   e. Who can help me?

This should serve as a guide to get you started. You will need to tailor it so that it reflects you and the specific areas you've decide to work on. The more you journal, the easier it gets.

As you work to incorporate journaling into your life, remember the mighty elephant is best eaten in small bites. Being patience and consistent are crucial in forming new habits. Begin writing perhaps three days a week, first thing in the morning or just before bed.

Learning to identify a variety of different emotions is a big part of cultivating your emotional intelligence. To help you dig a little deeper during journaling, here's a short list of feelings words from A to Z.

List of Emotions (Partial)

Amazed	Foolish	Overwhelmed
Angry	Frustrated	Peaceful
Annoyed	Furious	Proud
Anxious	Grieving	Relieved
Ashamed	Happy	Reluctant
Bitter	Hopeful	Resentful
Bored	Hurt	Sad
Comfortable	Inadequate	Satisfied
Confused	Insecure	Scared
Content	Inspired	Self-conscious
Depressed	Irritated	Shocked
Determined	Jealous	Silly
Discouraged	Joy	Stupid
Disgusted	Lonely	Suspicious
Eager	Lost	Tense
Embarrassed	Loving	Terrified
Empathetic	Miserable	Trapped
Energetic	Motivated	Uncomfortable
Envious	Nervous	Worried
Excited	Neglected	Worthless

■ ■ ■

"For news of the heart, ask the face."
— West African saying

Strategy #3

Purposeful Listening

In today's fast-pace organization, listening is key to effective working relationships among employees and between management and staff. Listening skills also impact a company's interaction with customers and other businesses. It is equally important in our personal life. Listening is key to all effective communication. Without the ability to listen effectively, messages are easily misunderstood.

Listening is the key to great relationships and understanding. It's important in today's society, with all of our high-tech communication capabilities, to tune in and really listen to one another whenever possible pays dividends. However, research shows that the average person listens at only about 25% efficiency.

A *purposeful* listener knows how to mirror the same energy or emotions as the speaker. Show that you're engaged by responding with matching expressions. Reflect their feelings by responding with a smile when they smile and nod when they're looking for clues that you're getting what they're saying to you.

Purposeful listening can help you diffuse conflict. There are times in the workplace or a personal relationship when you may have to deal with conflict. Although you may not always agree with other person's point of view, it's important to be open to the experiences and perspectives (*empathic listening*) of others, and the best way to demonstrate this is through purposeful listening.

Conflict between two parties can make people defensive, but if a person feels that their concerns are being listened to and taken seriously, the chances of reaching a resolution is high.

And, if both parties feel that their point or perspective is clearly understood, the resolution is likely to be longer lasting. It may also encourage the parties to speak regularly and openly about conflict, resulting in a more transparent workplace generally.

In October 2016 Inc.com published the below list of benefits of being a great listener.

1. Mutual trust: Authentic listening generates respect and trust between talker and listener. Employees will naturally respond better to managers who they think are listening intently to their needs.
2. Productivity: Problems are solved faster if people are encouraged to explain problems and be given the freedom to work though solutions out loud before being told what to do.
3. Cooler heads prevail: Listening intently helps both sides to stay cool -- and helps them cool off -- when they are dealing with a crisis or discussing a sensitive issue.
4. Boosts confidence: Great listeners tend to have better self-esteem and self-image because, in their listening, they work toward establishing positive relationships.
5. Fewer mistakes: Good listening leads to more accuracy in retaining information. You'll remember important facts later on, minimizing the risk of miscommunication and making mistakes.

Characteristics of a Purposeful Listener (Place a check mark by each that you routinely demonstrate)

- Is motivated
- Makes eye contact
- Shows interest
- Avoids distractions
- Has empathy
- Asks questions
- Paraphrases
- Doesn't over talk
- Is aware of and confronts biases

Listening is not a passive process. In fact, the listener can, and should, be at least as engaged in the process as the speaker.

It is important not to jump to conclusions (low impulse control) about what you see and hear. You should always seek clarification to ensure that your understanding is correct.

Listening Test

Examine the following statements and situations and indicate how you would most likely respond. In order to receive the most accurate results, please answer as truthfully as possible.

For each of the following questions, select the answer (√) that best describes your listening habits.			
	Usually	Sometimes	Seldom
1. Maintain eye contact with the speaker.			
2. I determine whether or not a speaker's ideas are worthwhile solely by his or her appearance and delivery			
3. I try to align my thoughts and feelings with those of the speaker.			
4. I listen for specific facts rather than for "the big picture".			
5. I listen for both factual content and the emotion behind the literal words			
6. I ask questions for clarification and understanding.			
7. I withhold judgement of what the speaker is saying until he or she is finished.			
8. I make a conscious effort to evaluate the logic and consistency of what is being said.			
9. While listening, I think about what I'm going to say as soon as I have my chance.			
10. I try to have the last word.			

Scoring Key and Interpretation.

For questions 1, 3, 5, 6, 7 and 8, give yourself 3 points for "Usually", 2 points for "Sometimes", and 1 point for "Seldom".

For questions 2, 4, 9, and 10, give yourself 3 points for "Seldom", 2 points for "Sometimes", and 1 point for "Usually".

Sum up your total points. A score of 27 or higher means you are a good listener. A score of 22 to 26 suggests you have some listening deficiencies. A score of less than 22 indicates that you have developed a number of bad listening habits.

■ ■ ■

There is a difference between listening and waiting for your turn to speak.
- Simon Sinek

Strategy #4

Meditation

Meditation is an approach to training the mind, similar to the way that fitness is an approach to training the body. In other words, meditation means turning your attention away from distracting thoughts and focusing on the present moment.

It often feels like there is just not enough time in the day to get everything done. We are often so busy we feel there is no time to stop and meditate! But meditation actually gives you more time by making your mind calmer and more focused.

For example, if we are forced to work with a colleague whom we dislike, we will probably become irritated and feel put upon, with the result that we will be unable to work with him or her efficiently and our time at work will become stressful and unrewarding.

You'll be happy to hear that you can meditate anywhere and at any time, allowing yourself to access a sense of tranquility and peace no matter what's going on around you.

If you have not tried meditation before (or even if you had) his meditation exercise is an excellent introduction to meditation techniques.

1. Sit or lie comfortably.

2. Close your eyes. Meditation can be performed with the eyes open or closed, however as a beginner it may be best to first try meditating with your eyes closed.

3. Breathe naturally. Make no effort to control the breath. Try to focus on your breathing and only your breathing. Don't *think* about your breathing or pass any sort of judgment of it (e.g. that breath was shorter than the last one),

4. Focus your attention on the breath and on how the body moves with each inhalation and exhalation. Notice the movement of your body as you breathe. Observe your chest, shoulders, rib cage, and belly. Simply focus your attention on your breath without controlling its pace or intensity. If your mind wanders, return your focus back to your breath.

Maintain this meditation practice for two to three minutes to start, and then try it for longer periods.

Meditation doesn't have to be limited to strictly defined practice sessions, you can also practice meditation throughout your day to day life. For example, in moments of stress, try to take a few seconds to focus solely on your breathing and empty your mind of any negative thoughts or emotions.

A former client I had that had anger issues said that he had a very short fuse – to the point of wanting to commit acts of violence. He was concerned that if it wasn't dealt with, he might lose his job. Meditation taught him to recognize his own anger and become more detached from it. It cleared his mind and calmed him down.

Meditation induces relaxation, which increases the compound nitric oxide that causes blood vessels to open up and subsequently, blood pressure to drop.

Here's a partial list of the physical and mental benefits of meditation:

- Lowers high blood pressure
- Lowers the levels of blood lactate, reducing anxiety attacks
- Decreases tension-related pain, such as, tension headaches, ulcers, insomnia,
- Increases serotonin production that improves mood and behavior
- Improves the immune system
- Increases the energy level
- Anxiety decreases
- Emotional stability improves
- Creativity increases
- Happiness increases
- Gain clarity and peace of mind
- Problems become smaller
- Sharpens the mind by increasing focus

Could you benefit from any of the above? Meditation just might be the strategy to implement.

Think of meditation as a form of mental hygiene - the same as if brushing your teeth, as you will. When you were young, you had to be trained to create the habit of teeth brushing. However, now that brushing is routine, the thought of not doing it is unthinkable.

The same goes for meditation - once you get into the habit and experience all of the mental clarity, emotional stability, physical relaxation that the practice offers, not practicing meditation seems unimaginable!

By training in meditation, we create an inner space and clarity that enables us to control our mind regardless of the external circumstances.

■ ■ ■

The right word may be effective, but no word was ever as effective as a rightly timed pause.

- Mark Twain

Strategy #5

Pause, Stop and Think

How many times have we passed judgement on others only to find that they had good reason for doing what they were doing or what they were saying? Everyone feels his perspective on a situation is right and everyone else is wrong. Like the employee that got upset with his boss because his boss called and gave him a project that needed to be completed before he went home – and it was 4:30! His immediate reaction? In a sign of exasperation, he pushed back from desk and threw his hands in the air and exclaimed "that's it!".

However, if he had a little patience, he would have waited to find out what his boss needed before getting angry.

Pausing is not a period. It is a moment in which we allow our mind a little time to organize our thoughts and even second guess our decisions.

The action of pressing PAUSE in our schedule requires a conscious thought to precede the action. The more we activate the response to pause, the more clearly we see just how necessary it is to develop a habit of pausing.

Isn't it odd that when there is more on the line, we stumble into the bad habit of "shooting from the hip" rather than giving full and measured consideration to our responsibilities?

I'll always remember the story of two lumberjacks who went into the woods. The first one went chopping down the trees for the whole day straight while the second one did some sawing and stopped during regular intervals. So, the first guy instinctively knew that his day's yield will be greater since he actually spent more time bringing down the trees.

Unfortunately, he was wrong. The second lumberjack came back with more timber pieces because when he stopped his cutting, he was taking the time to sharpen his saw.

While these strategies are just the tip of the iceberg in terms of developing your EI, putting them into practice will have you well on your way toward handling your emotions and relationships.

■ ■ ■

All learning has an emotional base.
                                    - Plato

Part 4: Summary

Chapter 7
PUTTING IT ALL
TOGETHER

Today's employers look for a lot of characteristics in an employee when they are interviewing. No longer is it a single skill. For example, it's nice if the candidate is dependable, has experience and education in the area of the job he or she will be doing, the interviewee is a quick learner, works well in a team, embraces diversity and inclusion and has a growth mindset.

There are many benefits to having emotional intelligent employees. Emotional intelligence has proven to make people work better with one another. Like other forms of intelligence, your emotional IQ is not a static trait. By learning your weaknesses and building upon your strengths, you can work toward greater emotional intelligence.

One of the greatest benefits of emotional intelligence, both within the workplace and in one's personal life, is the ability to maintain and display compassion for fellow humans. Compassion allows a person to connect with others on an emotional level.

Our emotional intelligence affects the quality of our lives because it influences our behavior and relationships. Taking time to reflect and examining why we decide to do what we do enables us to lead lives determined by our conscious intentions rather than circumstances alone.

Everyone wants to work with people who are easy to get along with, supportive, likeable, and can be trusted. Emotional intelligence is an important part of our social skills. What emotions do you struggle with? Developing your emotional intelligence requires time. Most of all it requires a serious examination of your emotional behavior, how you interact with others and recognizing areas you need to improve in.

We must learn to manage emotions the same way as we manage time, equipment, and other resources. Often our uncontrolled emotions are the product of stress that has been building up over time. Left unmanaged, our emotions can continue to fuel the feelings of stress, eventually leading to short tempers, angry words and unproductive activity. While we can't always control feelings of stress, we can and therefore should make an effort to control the disruptive emotions that they may trigger. Consider the following:

- Pay attention to your emotions. Don't ignore your emotions hoping that "out of sight is out of mind". Usually, the situation will remain until it's acknowledged. Our emotions are like the instrument panels on our cars – they tell us what's going on within.

- Determine the source of your feelings. Try to identify what brought these emotions to the surface. Was it stress, heavy workload, inappropriate comment someone made? Understand your responses and develop behaviors that allow you to be more objective.

- Realize that emotions are a part of the workplace. How many times have you heard someone say, "Leave your emotions at home!" It is unrealistic and impracticable to think that we can continue to conceal or ignore emotions and how they impact the work environment. Emotions such as joy, excitement, enthusiasm can be morale boosters which can raise productivity.

- Express your feelings in a non-confrontational manner. Don't play the "blame game" by making statements that blame others for what you are feeling – they will only become defensive. Instead use "I" statements that reflect what you are feeling. Do this: "I feel disappointed in receiving this report after the agreed upon due date". Instead of this: "You make me so upset when you're late with these reports".

- Maintain a neutral body and voice. By doing this, you will remain calm. Chances are this will have a similar effect on the other party – thus allowing for an opportunity for dialogue.

- Acknowledge the other party's feelings as legitimate. Remember, there are two sides to every coin. This means that just as you have feelings, so does the other party. And while you may not agree with them, they are as legitimate as yours – acknowledge them. It is more likely the other party will be more open to yours.

- Find and focus on the positives. Rather than asking what you don't like about the environment, ask people what they do like about it – be specific. Reinforce them. People are more willing to tackle what is wrong when they are being reinforced for what is right.

- Don't judge! Refrain from jumping to conclusion about what is being said - hear them out. If you agree or disagree with their point of view, it can be stated when all of the facts are in. Customers, coworkers, support staff, even bosses like to have their point heard – give them the chance.

- "Take Five". Request a "time out" when things get heated. This allows for regrouping emotionally and for reflection. Walk away from the situation. Removing yourself will enable both parties to regain their composure and control. It will also give you time to think about how you can best respond to whatever prompted the need to "take five". Set a reasonable time limit when both parties can agree to reconvene.

- Offer help when it's needed. When a difficult job has to be done, it might require you to "roll up your sleeves" and pitch in. Other times it might only require you to provide the needed resources or lend your knowledge. If you do nothing to help, your coworker, team or staff is likely to be annoyed. The stress of the task itself is made worse by the emotional feelings of abandonment.

- Be sure to treat everyone fairly. Set up and follow clear policies and procedures. Having rules in place minimizes emotional conflicts. When you treat people fairly, they tend to have mutual respect for each other, it promotes a team environment and it avoids the intent and appearance of unethical or compromising practices.

To effectively enhance your EI, there are four ability areas that I feel are critically important to be addressed. They are *listening, non-verbal communication, conflict management* and *stress management.* A wealth of information exists that expands the treatment of these topics beyond the scope of this book. I recommended that these sources be sought out and read as well.

It's not only in our professional lives where emotional intelligence matters, however, as it can be helpful in almost any interpersonal situation. Developing your emotional intelligence is important for personal, family and business relationships.

■ ■ ■

Dr. Hank's EQ Quiz

For each of the following items, rate how well you display the skill/ability described. Respond how you are, not how you should or want to be. Before responding, try to think of actual situations in which you have had the opportunity to use the ability. Use the following to select your best response:

Slight Skill/Ability = 1; Moderate Skill/Ability = 2, 3. 4; High Skill/Ability = 5

1	Know the impact that my behavior has on others.	
2	Calm myself quickly when angry.	
3	Build consensus with others.	
4	Identify when I experience mood shifts.	
5	Regroup quickly after a setback.	
6	Help others manage their emotions.	
7	Follow my words with actions.	
8	Engage in intimate conversations with others.	
9	Know when I become defensive.	
10	Calm myself quickly when I get angry or upset.	
11	Sensitive to other people's emotions and moods.	
12	I enjoy meeting and talking with people.	
13	I know what triggers my emotions.	
14	Can pull myself together quickly after a setback.	
15	I have good relationships with others.	

Total Score

Sum up your responses to the 15 statements to obtain your overall emotional intelligence score

The above quiz is an excerpt from the EISAP 2.0™

Scoring

This questionnaire provides an indication of your emotional intelligence. If you received a total score of:

- 40 or more, you have high level of emotional intelligence.
- 31 and above means you have a good platform of emotional intelligence from which to continue developing your skills.
- 30 and below indicates that you realize that you are probably below average in emotional intelligence.

No matter how high or low your score, you can increase your emotional intelligence by learning more about how you respond in various situations. Additionally, an increase in emotional intelligence can help you do better in your job and personal life.

* This was an EQ Quiz and is NOT meant to provide an accurate assessment of your EQ. An accurate assessment requires responding to the full EISAP 2.0™.

About the Author

- Founder and President of The HLC Group, Inc. training, coaching in Emotional Health and Wellbeing
- Founder and CEO of the <u>Society of Emotional Intelligence</u>
- Emotional Intelligence Coach to leaders and organizations.
- Certified Hypnotherapist
- Anger Management Specialist
- Conference and Workshop Speaker
- Training Partner of MHS (Multi Health Systems) where he certifies individuals in the use of the EQ-i 2.0 – the most widely used validated assessment on emotional intelligence in the market today.
- Author of several books on emotional intelligence
- Radio show host of The Dr. Hank Show. Heard weekly at 12:00 noon EST - <u>blogtalkradio.com/thedrhankshow</u>

Services Available

Dr. Hank can serve as a speaker and/or workshop facilitator for your conference, retreat, or meeting. An engaging speaker, he has a skill for connecting with audiences and helping them go beyond simply listening to what he has to say, to implementing the concepts and techniques he speaks about. He primarily speaks on the following topics but will certainly tailor his presentation and/or training for your event:

- ➤ Emotional Intelligence
- ➤ Emotional Health and Wellbeing
- ➤ Leadership
- ➤ Diversity and Inclusion

Other books by the author on Emotional Intelligence
- Could your Emotional Intelligence be Holding You Back?
- 21 Ways to Improve your Emotional Intelligence

Since 1987, the HLC Group, Inc. has been designing and delivering training interventions aimed at performance improvement and culture change. Seminars and coaching services include:

- Executive Coaching
- Anger Management
- Emotional Health and Wellbeing
- Developing your Emotional Intelligence

Its broad client base includes private and public-sector agencies. The firm is located in Tampa, FL.

Recommended Assessments

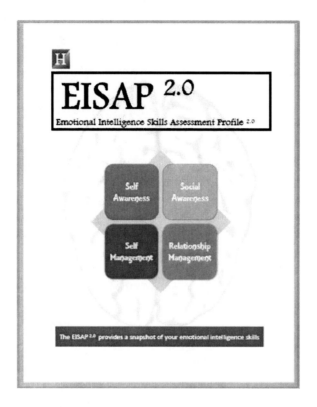

EISAP 2.0™ - Call to order: 813-431-9786

EQ-i 2.0™ – Call to order or be certified: 813-431-9786

NOTES

NOTES

NOTES

Additional copies of this book can be purchased by contacting:

The HLC group, Inc.
PO Box 341453
Tampa, FL 33694
813.431-9786
www.societyofei.org
http://www.hlcgroupinc.com/
thehlcgroup@gmail.com

CPSIA information can be obtained
at www.ICGtesting.com
Printed in the USA
FFOW01n2354220718
47515505-50887FF